NEIL M. JUSTIN

YOU CAN AND WILL FULFILL YOUR PURPOSE.

ISBN: 978-1-953788-81-8

INTRODUCTION

Dreams.

Visions.

Purpose.

Goals.

Assignments.

These are words that I typically use to describe what we want to do in life or the things we know we were born to do. When I was a small child, I dreamed of being a pilot. As I grew older, I started to nurture a second dream, which was to serve God in ministry. So, by the time I graduated from college, I had two dreams.

At first, I thought those two dreams were competing against each other, so I believe I was in a dilemma for wanting to do both things with almost the same level of passion. But during a graduation service that the church that I grew up in was having for all of the graduates that year, we were seated on the stage, and each graduate was given a minute to share what school they were graduating from, what degree they had, and what they wanted to do with their life.

So, I sat on that stage, asking God which of those two dreams He wanted me to do. I told Him I felt like I had to choose between the two. I said to the Lord, "Whatever you want me to do, I will do it. Whether You want me to pursue my career in aviation and fly, or You want me to just give up everything and serve in ministry full-time."
I was ready to give up one for the other, whichever dream was God's desire for me.

But the Lord said to me in the form of a question, "Why not do both?"

At that moment, I got the vision of combining aviation and ministry as my life's goal. I understood that my life's purpose was centered around both dreams. And that, beloved, is the crux of this book.

So, you're getting all of me, the entirety of Neil Justin. I am a pastor and an airline pilot. I've served as an assistant pastor for five years, up until the point of this writing – four years at my previous ministry and one year after I got married at the church pastored by my wife's parents.

I've experienced the best of aviation and ministry and the worst of both worlds. Ministry does have its dark moments. Ministry can be frustrating at times. And as much as I enjoy flying, becoming and remaining an airline pilot is definitely not an easy road.

So, my journey of combining and succeeding in both worlds has never been the smoothest of my experiences. There have been moments that I've experienced where my dreams could have been destroyed, and I've had times when the only option I had before me was to give up and let one or both dreams die. But here I am, still standing strong and doing all the Lord has for me. This is the purpose of this book.

For you to have picked up this book, I bet you may have experienced moments where you knew what you wanted to do with your life. But something happened, and the passion for your dream got dampened until it disappeared. You may have even had several dreams and goals at different points in your life, but you've given up on them, and they are now abandoned or all over the place.

Maybe life simply happened to you. Maybe specific things from specific people or situations rammed into your life and devastated you so much that your dreams, purpose, and that assignment you believed in with all your heart have been dashed. You don't think that you can do anything with your life anymore. Rather than choosing to live (to your fullest), you just decide to exist.

You may have also had terrible experiences that sapped energy out of your life, and you no longer have the passion to go after your dreams and visions as you should. This book will help you see that it is not God's plan for you to simply exist. It is not His plan that your purpose gets destroyed. It is not God's will that the dreams He put in your heart should die and never get accomplished.

God came through Jesus so that you would have life and have it more abundantly. God came so that you can live. Why?

Just as an eagle was born to soar high up in the sky. Just as an airplane has been built to fly high in the sky. You, too, have been born for a specific purpose. And that purpose is meant to be fulfilled.

So, I want you to live, not merely exist or survive. But more importantly, God wants you to live. He wants you to achieve every dream He has given to you. God wants you to fulfill your purpose because He has created you to live.

The Bible is filled with messages to help us live to soar. Throughout this book, we will use several scriptural references. Ezekiel 37, which is the story of the Valley of Dry Bones, is one of them. We will consider some truths from it and draw some principles to solidify your determination to live and live to soar – to live for your purpose and to live to fulfill that dream you may have not yet discovered or even given up on. This book is designed to help you awaken your dead or forgotten dreams and live life to the fullest.

I invite you to read. I invite you to take notes. I invite you to **LIVE TO SOAR**. Let's go!

SECTION 1
Live

CHAPTER 1

SECTION 1
THE VALLEY OF DRY BONES

"The hand of the LORD was upon me, and carried me out in the spirit of the LORD, and set me down in the midst of the valley which was full of bones, and caused me to pass by them round about: and, behold, there were very many in the open valley; and, lo, they were very dry."
Ezekiel 37:1-2 KJV

Ezekiel 37:1-2 talks about the vision God gave Ezekiel, the Prophet. He says that the spirit of the Lord took him in a vision and set him in a valley. And in this valley is a pile of dead men's bones. I need you to note how this scripture was careful to say that the bones were **scattered** and **very dry.**

And then God asks him, 'Son of man, can these dry bones live? 'And Ezekiel's response to Him was, 'Oh Lord, thou knowest? '

Let's look at that for a second.

These bones, as you would see later on in the story, were all part of a vast army of people. In other words, these bones all had a specific linkage or specific connection to form specific bodies and people. They had in themselves what was needed to make a battle-ready army.

In our lives, these bones can represent our dreams and life's goals. They can represent the culmination or the complete picture of our dreams and goals. Just as we put the pieces together to a puzzle to get a full picture, our dreams and goals make up the entirety of our lives. And the bones in this story, once they are put together, represent the complete picture of not just one person but an entire army.

In your lifetime, there may have been dreams that you had, visions that you caught, and goals you aspired to achieve. But something could have happened to cause those dreams to feel scattered and unreachable, and you may have given up on them. You may have succumbed to situations that turned your dreams into dead, dry bones. But just as in the story of Ezekiel, even the dry bones are not a dead end.

They can live again. Your dreams can come alive again. You can live.

Let me tell you my story.

A YOUNG BOY BURNING WITH PASSION

From when I was about four years old, my passion for flying was already ignited. I remember moving to the island of St. Lucia, where my parents were originally from. They sent me to live in St. Lucia for two years when I turned five years old. And the house I lived in was on a hill that overlooks the Northern airport (of the two airports in St. Lucia). So, from the house, I could effortlessly see planes come and go.

I remember vividly that it didn't matter what I was doing; I would always stop everything to watch every plane that moved around the airport. It didn't matter if I was playing with my neighbors. If I was eating inside. If I was just outside the house. If I was doing homework or even watching T.V. Whenever a plane was landing or taking off, and I could hear it, I'd stop whatever I was doing, and I would either run to the window if I was inside the house or I would stand on the porch if I was outside just to see that plane come or go.

The airport was also adjacent to a decent beach. It's not the best beach on the island, but it's my favorite for obvious reasons. It was right beside the airport,

so it was definitely my favorite spot. I would go to that beach when it was time for recreation or whenever I just wanted to take some time off and relax. I remember that I always enjoyed the waves and the sand. But what I remarkably enjoyed the most about the beach was that it kept me in close proximity to that runway so I could watch the planes take off and land.
You already know what I dreamed of becoming later in life.

Absolutely, a pilot. Obviously, the passion I had for airplanes implied that I couldn't see myself doing anything other than flying them.

Fast forward to my 18th birthday; while I was in college, I did my first flight – my introductory flight –and was super excited. I couldn't put a name to the kind of emotions that overwhelmed me at that point. I knew this was something that I wanted to do. I didn't want to do anything else outside aviation.

I went to Aviation High School, which has a fantastic aircraft maintenance program. I graduated from high school with flying colors. But I didn't want to fix planes. I wanted to fly them.

Fast forward now to graduating from college. At this point, I am now saved, having accepted Christ as my Lord and Savior in church several years ago.

I moved back to the United States when I was seven. From the age of seven until now, I have not only received Christ into my life, but I have also become passionately involved in ministry. I started playing the drums. I went from drums to singing in choirs. I then transitioned to playing the keyboard.

Soon enough, I also started going on mission trips. I've gone on several mission trips in the Caribbean and Africa. Canada and South Florida in the United States are also not left out. I've spent a sizeable portion of my life on mission trips to several places.

I delved deeperinto ministry, and I involved myself in numerous activities like playing music, singing, acting in dramas, preaching, and visiting prisons, nursing homes, and hospitals. I also did not mind talking about God on the street corners or in the subway. I've also been a part of two album recordings.

In a nutshell, ministry had become another burning passion of mine. So, you can already start to guess how many dilemmas I faced when I graduated from college in 2003 – I had two things I did not mind pouring my life into.

Little did I know that my passions would be badly tampered with. Something happened in my life, and it sort of temporarily put my passions on hold.

In 2008, I met a woman and got into a relationship with her. At that point, my aviation career had already started taking off. I had been working as an airline pilot for two years, so I supposed a serious relationship was not out of place.

It was a long-distance relationship. So, I was cautious at first because I had been in a relationship before, and it hadn't worked out. I kept praying and asking God when this would happen for me. When I saw that my life was coming together in terms of my career and I was already set up with this young woman (she really had my attention and was able to tug on my heartstrings), I felt this was really it. And I wanted to be married to her.

So, we got engaged in the summer of that year. But by the fall, the relationship was over. I was devastated. Never would I have thought things would end – and do so quickly. A lot of things did happen, some of which were mostly my fault. But the breakup came as a complete shock to me.

When I realized that the relationship was over (with the ring returned to me) and there was nothing I could do to remedy the situation, I got on a plane heading back home. I thought the breakup was the scariest thing that happened to me that season. But within an hour after take-off, I wanted to get off the airplane.

That frightened me so much because, before that point, it didn't matter what was going on in my life; flying was a source of solace to me. It was my comfort spot, and I enjoyed it very much. I always literally felt a piece of it because I enjoyed being in control of a plane and taking in the view outside. But none of that mattered to me at that point because I was heartbroken.

All I just wanted to do was to give up on everything.

When I landed, I quickly went to the chief pilot's office and told him I needed to take some time off. Without going into too much detail, I let him know that I had just suffered a broken relationship and needed some time to get myself together.

He understood and said, 'Take all the time you need.' He went ahead to clear my schedule for the rest of the month. I went home and sunk into depression for several days.

I didn't want to talk to anyone – not even God. I was so upset with Him. After all I had done in ministry – preaching, going for missions, and writing numerous blogs that edified and encouraged – I couldn't believe God would let me go through such horrible heartbreak.

One thing I'd love to point out here is that despite being upset with God, I did not try to hide how I felt. And this is what He wants from us – openness, no matter the situation. God knows when you are upset with him, so just be honest in time. And He understands you better than you think. He does. His love is amazing. You never want to hold back and miss experiencing His love.

So, my dreams and aspirations for life were scattered by a single heartbreak – just as those bones were left dry in the valley. And at that time, I felt I could never do anything with my life again. I felt dead and without a purpose for my life.

It All Came Together

Fast forward to today, those passions have not only returned, but I've also further advanced in my assignments as an airline pilot in my career and in ministry. With the help of God and the many things He opened my eyes to see, every piece of my passions that got torn apart in different directions was put together to result in the victorious life I now live.

In the process of this advancement, I've learned many lessons that I will generously share in subsequent chapters.

But... back to you.

What have you experienced that has caused your dreams to scatter? What have you gone through that may have caused you to want to lay down your assignments, goals, and passions because you think there's no way to achieve them anymore?

When I got married... Oh, by the way, I did get married to someone else, for whom I am so grateful to God. When I got married, one of the things that my brother, who was my best man, said during the reception was that he was so proud of me as his brother. But that was not all. He said that out of all of us who grew up together – friends, siblings, family members – and all of us who knew each other from a young age, I was literally the only one who eventually achieved the dreams I've nursed all my life. He explained that the rest had dreams but had never come close to achieving them.

My brother may have thought of that conversation as one of those emotional sibling conversations that usually happen during weddings. But for me, it was a powerful testimony, and it blessed me so much.

I believe that just as in the story in Ezekiel 37, where the bones ended up coming together, and the army came to life, your dreams can actually come back to life again. As a matter of fact, you are reading this book because God has not given up on you. So, you shouldn't give up either.

Even if you have given up on your dreams at any point, you can pick them right back up again. Those formerly dead dreams can reconnect, and the full picture of your vision, purpose, and assignment can come back to life.

Do you know why?

The end of that story was that an entire army had risen up in that valley, an exceeding great army. It wasn't just bones connecting to form a human. It wasn't just bones connecting to form a man and a woman. It was bones connecting to form an army of people, which meant that it wasn't just a group of people but a group of people with a specific purpose.

You have a purpose, too, just as that army had a purpose, to fight wars, secure, provide security, defend, and win. And there is a world waiting for your purpose to be realized and accomplished. I believe that will happen for you.

HOW DID THAT HAPPEN?
What killed your dreams?

How did you go from having a heart burning so much to achieving something or becoming someone to not even wanting to think about those dreams?

What sapped the life out of your dreams that they became as dry, lifeless, and scattered as those bones God showed Ezekiel?

What could have caused your dream to not only die but to become so dry that accomplishing it seems totally impossible?

There is a myriad of reasons that life can present to you, and each of these reasons is designed to automatically push you to quit.

But let's be on the same page, shall we?

When I say 'your dream,' I'm not talking about just a relationship goal you have. I'm not talking about your plans to keep yourself from being fired from a job. I'm not merely talking about your intentions to buy a house or a car.

But I am referring to the crux of your existence. The reason you are here. The mission that God has and wants you to be a part of. Your purpose and the reason for your life.

What is it that has caused your dream to be dry, to be scattered, and seemingly unachievable?
I'll share a few things that could cause your dreams and visions to die.

Word Curses

More often than not, wrong words or word curses are the reason most dreams never see the light of day.

And the dangerous thing about word curses is that they often come from people we love and respect. They come as words that keep us safe, help us stay logical, or temporarily remove the fear of what we do not know. They come as something someone who has influence over your life says to you. And when you hear those words, they sound more believable than what God has for you.

Someone – especially people you hold in high esteem – could say things to you that can take your heart away from the things God has shown you and that He has for you. That happens because we can sometimes get so carried away by our act of honor for the men in our lives that their words may start meaning more to us than the Word of God.

What someone who has influence over your life has said may have caused your mind to abandon what you believe God has for you to do.

Consequently, you buried your dreams because you stopped believing they could be achieved.

Let me tell you how the wrong words almost derailed me from what God has for me. This one's on the ministry side, but it's more recent.

Before I got married, I met this young, beautiful young woman. My wife's name is Shirley. I am so grateful for her. But we almost did not get married. And that was because of the influence of someone's words in my life.

I had been serving in a church for twelve years as a minister of music and for four years as an associate pastor. That church, that ministry, was my family. I loved them. I loved the senior pastor. I loved his family.

I still do.

When I met my wife, it was under a unique, God-ordained experience. My wife slides in my D.M. occasionally, but I didn't initially pay much attention to her.

Then, one day, while at work (as an airline pilot, remember?), I was walking to the gate when she came to my mind. She didn't just come to mind for me to go on her social media, look her up, and look at some pictures. I needed to check on her – with a bit of urgency. I sensed something might be wrong.

So, without asking the Lord any questions, I quickly grabbed my phone while walking to the gate, sent her a quick message in her D.M., and said, 'Hey, for some reason, God wanted me to check on you. So, I wanted to see how you were doing.'

Well, she thought I was spitting. She thought I was just trying to strike a random conversation but using a spiritual connotation. But I was serious. This was my pastoral side, and I knew it was no joke.

It turned out that there was something that she was experiencing in her church that was a little frustrating to her, and she needed the air of someone who would listen.

We met, and I listened to her air some of her concerns. Immediately she was done, the Lord gave me a word, not just for her, but for her parents.

I knew it was God doing His thing all along because the previous year, I had received a word from someone who said to me that I had to stop searching for the right woman, that the person who would end up being my wife was related to the assignment that I have. The person further said that there was a specific assignment that I had to do, and my wife would be waiting for me on that assignment.

So, when I met my wife, I didn't immediately think she was the one. But I did have questions for God. After our meeting, I completed the assignment, talked to the Lord about her, and we became friends. Little did I know that our friendship would turn into a full-blown relationship. And it did not take long for me to realize that she was definitely the one.

I proposed to my wife within seven months, and another four months later, we were getting married.

But we almost didn't get married because someone that I valued and respected very much felt that marrying my wife was not the Lord's will for me. He put me in a position where I had to make a choice between marrying her and fulfilling my life's purpose.

I was told that my wife would cost me my pilot's license and career. I was told that she would dominate my life so much that it would rob me of the assignment of God on my life. In other words, he made me believe that if I marry my wife, my life and future will be destroyed.

I listened to him because I valued him so much and wanted to preserve my relationship with him as a spiritual cover and father. I decided to end the relationship with her.

But when I ended the relationship, I was so heartbroken and in pain because I really knew she was God's will for me. So, I reached a point where I had to decide between going for what God was saying to me or what I thought God was saying to me through someone I respected.

Thankfully, I recovered from that influence and decided to go through with the marriage, marrying one of the most beautiful women in the world, both inside and out.

On my wedding day, as my wife walked down the aisle to the front with her parents in hand, the presence of God was so strong in that sanctuary. I instantly knew without doubt that God's hands and peace were on my marriage. And I was so grateful that I obeyed God and could host His presence at my wedding as I do in my marriage.

A word curse, something that someone says to you, can carry so much weight in your life that it can cause you to abort what you want to do. And the sad thing is that you may not realize when word curses are working against your dreams until their effects start to show.

Self-Sabotage

Self-sabotage can also make you lose your dreams and the things God has for you.

You may have made intentional or unintentional mistakes in the past or made decisions that did not yield the best outcomes for you. Whether you were misinformed or made your best-informed decision that sabotaged your plans and caused things in your life not to go the way they should go.

You may have seemingly aborted your destiny and purpose by your deeds and how you viewed life. You may have placed a stumbling block before your assignment as a result of something you did, said, or chased after. You may have also given in to a distraction or a deviation that pushed you away from your path of purpose.

And all these now make you believe there is really nothing left for you to do with your life. Those mistakes and their ripple effects can also kill your visions and dreams and make them seem unachievable. They can sap the life out of all those aspirations you've had over the years.

Victimization

When you deal with victimization or you witness the victimization of other people, it can shatter your dreams and leave you hopeless.

Victimization can happen when the circumstances around your life make you appear as though you are disadvantaged or not as lucky as other people. Then, you start to think negative thoughts about yourself, you begin to look down on or think less of those high things you hoped to achieve, and you also start to feel that you have no control over the things that happen to you – especially bad things.

When the effects of victimization continue in your life, you will hardly have any space to accommodate your dreams. And in no time, they start to die off.

Impostor Syndrome

The last one on my list is impostor syndrome.

You can do it. You can achieve those dreams and aspirations. You have what it takes to succeed, realize your dream, and manifest the word in your life. But you don't think you deserve it. You don't think you're worthy of it. You don't believe you are made to have your dreams come to pass. You think you're an imposter and a fraud, and people will eventually find out.

And because of that feeling, you end up aborting your purpose and destiny. Because you believe you are not significant enough to fulfill that purpose God has for you, and so you take the energy and life out of your dreams and visions.

But It's Coming Back Together

There are myriads of reasons people give up and let their dreams die and dry up, like the bones in the book of Ezekiel, and yours may not even be among the ones I talked about. But irrespective of what may have happened to your dreams, they can still live again.

If your dreams die because you believed something someone said to you, those words are not the final say, and your dreams can live again. If your dreams died because of a mistake you made or a bitter experience you had, remember that the God who gave you that dream is a merciful

Genesis 2:4-7 KJV

Breath

Brood over this Word a little bit. And as you do that, try to picture the role the breath from God plays in our lives as people created by God.

The original word for breath is a Hebrew word pronounced nishama, a feminine noun meaning breath. It means wind, and it also means spirit. Its meaning also parallels two other Hebrew words. One of them is the word nephesh. If you've followed some of the well-known teachers of scripture on TV or social media, I'm pretty sure you would have heard them use nephesh when they talk about the spirit. Then the other word is ruach, which also means spirit.

All of these words describe the word breath. And by definition, breath for humans is recognized as the source and center of life. So, it is safe to say that if you do not have breath in you, you're not alive (obviously?!).

But can I put it to you (just as we have seen from Genesis 2) that breath itself has a source?

Our breath as humans – the thing that makes us living souls, the seed of our living – comes from God. So, breath is what gives us life, but it comes from God. This also means that God can choose to withhold life by withholding breath from humanity. Therefore, people's breath (and the need for a life source from Another) symbolizes their weakness and frailty.

Unfortunately, the reason most people never get to truly live is not really that God withheld life from them. Instead, it is because they fail to recognize where (from Whom) the seed for our lives is sourced. We often put so much weight on the resources we are given instead of the source. And we miss it when we start to look for the foundation and reason for living from anything other than the One who gives life. This is why Adam and Eve were tempted and ate from the Tree of Knowledge of Good and Evil instead of going for the Tree of Life. They did not understand the value of the Source.

When you feel mistreated or abused, or you feel like the situation you are in is toxic, or people or situations come at you in ways that do not value who you really are, it is usually because there's a lack of real understanding of who you are. When you fail to recognize the Source of your life, you are bound to misunderstand and abuse your life's purpose. As Miles Monroe would always say, anytime you do not understand the real purpose of a thing, abuse is inevitable.

When we do not fully understand who God is to us, we do not look to put Him first when it comes to prayer, so we fail to put him first as the foundation of our lives. We'll be quick to go to other things instead of going to God unless we are in trouble because we are taking God for granted. But God is the source of your life.

Therefore, we must understand that before we can begin to live life to its fullest, we should first receive and recognize the seed that is required. And this seed, as we have seen, comes from the breath of God.

GOD HAS GIVEN TO EVERY MAN A MEASURE OF FAITH.
His Word over your life and purpose.

Now, it isn't just that God breathed into man the breath of life. Yes, he did breathe into him. But you got to remember, *man does not live by bread alone, but by every word that proceeds out of the mouth of God.*

So, what that means then is it's not just breath that God is throwing at you. It's also His Word that is coming at you. It is also His essence. The Word of God is the spirit of God.

God's Word is the source of your dreams, passions, and assignments. I know we put a lot of weight on the assignment. Still, one of the dangers of putting too much weight on a person's assignment is that they might equate their assignment to their identity, which is not supposed to be so. The Bible doesn't say that God breathed into man the breath of life, and immediately, man started to work. No, he first became a living soul. This means his identity was established from what was breathed out of God and into him.

What God says about you is your identity. Not just the assignment. Not just your career, what you're going to do in life, and how you're going to make an impact in the world. All of those are important. But what's more important is who you are. What God says about you is who you are.

Your future comes from the mouth of God. Your identity comes from the mouth of God. Your purpose comes from the mouth of God. Who you are exists from the mouth of God. Everything about you comes from the mouth of God. He determined when you were to be born, the sex you were going to be, who your parents were going to be, and what your environment was going to be like because He is particular about who you are on earth. You existed in the mind of God before you were even born. When you took your first breath, everything God said about you came into existence.

David understood the importance of God's Word for his life. He saw how his entire life depended on God's Word, and all through his writings in the book of Psalms, he makes clear how much he loves and continually craves that word. Now, this is the posture we need to have if we're going to succeed in life, if we're going to be clear on our identity, get that career advancement, get that promotion, be successful with that business venture, be successful in that area of ministry, or be successful in our families as husbands, wives, or parents. Whatever measure of success we ever want to achieve in any area of our lives, we will need the Word of God.

When you think about Ezekiel 37, the story of the Valley of Dry Bones, it was the word of the Lord that was released over those bones. Once the word was released, the Bible says there was a shaking, and the bones started coming together. Through His Word, God is going to put your life back together. It does not matter how many times you've had to feel parts of you are all over the place – your dream is over here, or your assignment is dashed over there. You've tried to do things, but it just seems like everything has fallen apart and is not working out. A word from God is all you need.

But that's not all.

A word from God can also reverse any seeming finality of any situation or circumstance that is your reality right now. A word from the Lord – a breath out of His mouth, is able to restore, is able to cause you to come alive, is able to cause your dream to come alive.

If you've given up on your dream or assignment, if you're wondering if this is going to go on, or maybe you're trying to hold on to a lesser version of your dream instead of what God specifically told you for your life, take this paragraph as a confirmation that a word from the Lord can reverse every single finality. It does not matter what may be the reason for the valley of dry bones you currently experience in your life; a word breathed out of God's mouth is what you need.

The right environment for the word to respond and produce.

When you receive the breath of God that makes you a living soul and His Word that frames the entirety of your existence, those are only the foundation of living and the parts God gets to play to help us truly live. When God has completed His part, whether we live or not will then depend on how well we play our part.

These are the generations of the heavens and of the earth when they were created, in the day that the LORD God made the earth and the heavens, and every plant of the field before it was in the earth, and every herb of the field before it grew: for the LORD God had not caused it to rain upon the earth, and there was not a man to till the ground. And the LORD God took the man, and put him into the garden of Eden to dress it and to keep it. Genesis 2:4-5,15 KJV

Looking at the scripture in Genesis 2:4-5,8, we see that before God created the plants, there was no man to till the ground. Then, when God formed man and planted the garden of Eden, He put man in the garden to tend it. And if you take a closer look at the entire chapter, you'll see that God planted every tree and plant man would need before putting him in the garden.

If, after, say, two years, Adam started to complain to God about food shortage and how the plants were no longer springing up on their own to feed him, would that be God's fault?

No, it won't. God already completed His part. It would be left for Adam to truly tend the garden, i.e., make the environment right for the plants to produce.

Don't worry. The part you get to play does not need you to create anything as God did. God will not ask of us what is beyond our ability, and the glory of creation belongs to God and God alone. So, all that is required of you is that you give a response to the breath and Word of God given to you. And that response has to do with making your environment right for the breath and Word of God given to you to truly produce life. Just as Adam had to continue to till the ground and tend the garden for the plants

Mark 5:35-36 KJV

Someone comes to discourage the ruler with the news of his daughter's death. Clearly, this discouragement came not because the messenger did not believe in Jesus's ability to heal the sick girl but because he felt the situation had gotten bigger than what Jesus's power could handle and that the girl had reached the end of the road. This is what discouragement does – it makes you doubt God's Word and be unable to experience the life in every word God speaks into your life.

Basically, he was saying Jesus was too late.

But can I tell you something?

Death is not a finality in your life. Death is only a transition into eternity as it relates to human beings. Just as Paul explained in his letters to the Thessalonians, when a believer – someone who believes in Jesus Christ, believes in what Jesus has done for their lives – dies, we are not hopeless because we know we're going to see them again. They're not going into eternal punishment but eternal life with God. So, death is not something we need to be afraid of. It isn't even supposed to act as a discouragement to us because Jesus was never discouraged by the news of the girl's death.

Instead, I want you to notice Jesus's response to the discouraging news the messenger brought – as I've underlined above.

It may feel so final that what God has said about you and your purpose is not going to happen because all the times you had a glimmer of hope, it got shattered. And that is the trick of the enemy – to get you hopeless. Your situation may seem dire, your circumstance may feel like the wasting of sickness, and you're begging God to fix your situation, your relationship, your job situation, and your school situation. But do not give up hope because here's the word of the Lord to you: **Be not afraid. Only believe.** Do not be afraid of the seeming finality of any situation you're going through. Only believe.

Be not afraid of what?

Be not afraid of the message you just heard. In other words, Jesus was telling him not to be discouraged from believing the Word of God. He expected Jesus to breathe into his daughter.

And He is saying the same thing to you today. Do not be discouraged from dwelling on God's Word that has been breathed into you. Sure enough, there are words or messages that may have been screaming at you. Those messages have been trying to discourage you by screaming at you about your situation and what you're currently going through. It may seem so final that your dreams, purpose, and the things that God said He would do through your life may never happen.

But I want you to take your focus off all those threats. Surround yourself with people who encourage you to pay attention to God's Word and produce fruits that align with the Word of God breathed into you, just as we would see Jesus do shortly.

And when he was come in, he saith unto them, Why make ye this ado, and weep? the damsel is not dead, but sleepeth. And they laughed him to scorn. But when he had put them all out, he taketh the father and the mother of the damsel, and them that were with him, and entereth in where the damsel was lying. And he took the damsel by the hand, and said unto her, Talitha Kumi; which is, being interpreted, Damsel, I say unto thee, arise. And straightway the damsel arose, and walked; for she was of the age of twelve years. And they were astonished with a great astonishment.
Mark 5:39-42 KJV

Next, Jesus gets to the ruler's house, and another round of discouragement is thrown at them. The people laughed at Jesus to scorn when He said the girl was not dead.

But what did Jesus do? He already knew that He had the power to raise the dead girl. But He still had to create the right environment for God's Word (and breath that will later go into the girl) to produce by eliminating discouragement and doubt. So, Jesus sends everyone else out, except her parents and His disciples – people who had enough faith for God's breath to bring about the girl's healing.

Exposure to what ignites your vision.

But strong meat belongeth to them that are of full age, even those who by reason of use have their senses exercised to discern both good and evil.
Hebrews 5:14 KJV

This Bible verse probably has no direct relationship with what we are trying to establish in this chapter. But I want you to see how the Bible puts emphasis on how consistent practice guarantees perfection so that we can understand how constantly exposing ourselves to things and people that ignite passion in us can help the seed of God's Word respond and produce in our lives.

So, here are some things that can ignite your vision - God's Word over your life – when you expose yourself to them:

A dream

Like in my story, which I shared in the introduction and first chapter, a dream (or vision, passion, or assignment) is a vehicle through which God's Word over us can produce results.

When we have dreams and passions, it is our way of holding on to fragments of who God ordained that we should become at the time He created us. And when we continue to nurture those dreams, as I did by going to aviation school and serving in ministry (as a drummer and missionary), we make it possible for God's Word over us to yield results.

A problem that stirs a desire

When we go through tough times, trying times, or seasons that make us question God's love for us, those seasons are not always there to break us. While you are in the experience, it may seem so. But when you look at the bigger picture, you may find that some problems we experience are simply there to stir up a desire in us. Some challenges are just there to stir the waters of desire in you so that you can decide and commit to choosing God's Word over and over again.

Maybe you just need to see something through that challenge you're facing. And when you eventually see that thing, it will spur you to choose God's Word and live. It will spur you to start to use God's gift and provision in your life to solve the problems confronting you. It will empower you to become the best version of yourself, which you never knew existed.

You'll be a person doing what you are called to do.

Another way you can create the right environment for the Word of God spoken over you to produce is by placing yourself around people (or a person) doing what you are called to do.

It's so powerful!

Do you know why? Seeing and being around someone who is currently living in the future God has shown you has a way of breaking down barriers of impossibilities that may want to hold you back. It just tells you that if this person could do it, then you too can. If God can use them the way He is doing, then He surely can use you too. If the same word God breathed into them is yielding and producing tremendous results, then it can do the same in your life, too.

This is the reason Elisha was able to walk in the prophetic anointing as much as he did. He had seen God do wonders through his master, Elijah. And so, when the mantle was passed to him, he had no mountain of doubt or impossibilities to deal with.

An invention that sparks an idea.

As mundane as this may sound, inventions by other people can also awaken something in us. We can use, see, or experience the work of other people, and it will make us realize how we have also been empowered by God's breath to create things that solve some of the problems people encounter around us.

Something natural and invigorates your imagination.

Some Christians may believe that being led by God's Spirit has nothing to do with our imaginations. But God can use our imaginations to create the right environment for the visions He places on our hearts.

Just by creatively engaging the faculties of your imagination, you can explore things about your future that you probably never imagined were possible.

And I have noticed that being close to nature invigorates my creativity and turns on those imaginative switches in my mind. I believe engaging with nature every now and then can work the same wonder on you, too.

But God did not give up on us. While He still did not take away man's freewill, we see again in Deuteronomy 30:19 I call heaven and earth to record this day against you, that I have set before you life and death, blessing and cursing: therefore choose life, that both thou and thy seed may live:

God, again, presented life and death, blessing and cursing to the children of Israel, and even convinced them to choose life so that they would live.

Today, He still presents that choice to us, to choose between life and death, between living and dying, and between having the will to live or leaving our lives, dreams, and assignments to die. God is placing before you life and death, blessing and curse, and He is hoping you will go for life. God wants you **to choose** to live that life He has made available for us in Jesus Christ. He wants you **to choose** to allow His Word, His breath, to breathe life into those dreams and passions so you can live to life's fullest.

Your Purpose

The Lord is not slack concerning his promise, as some men count slackness; but is longsuffering to us-ward, not willing that any should perish, but that all should come to repentance.
2 Peter 3:9 KJV

Now, we understand the context of what Peter was talking about. But there's something specific in there that I want to get to, and that's the word *willing*. The Greek word used there has meaning in several ways. From a human standpoint, it could mean a desire, wish, and goal. But when it's used specifically with respect to God, it has a passive connotation to it, which is why it speaks more of an internal desire. But the way God operates is that what his desire is, the thing that pleases him, leads him to act. So there's another word that is used for willing or will that involves a more active role. *When it says here that the Lord is not willing that any should perish, but that all should come to repentance*, it talks about the desire of God, the plan of God, or the mission of God. The desire is what is internal, but then it becomes a mission that leads God to act so that everybody has access to come to repentance.

What does this have to do with us as it relates to the will to live?

You see, as I mentioned earlier, God made the first move. When it comes to your purpose, life's plan, and gifts, God invested those in you. Making the first move shows that He really wants you to live. We talked about the scripture in the Book of Deuteronomy, where Moses was saying, I've set before you life and death, blessing and cursing. Choose life that you may live. In other words, I'm giving you a hint of which direction I want you to go. God, speaking through Moses, is saying he wants us to live, which means that God desires for you and me to live.

Our passions, desires, and goals all represent our will to live. One way to determine your passions is by finding out what excites you. For me, I've always wanted to be a pilot and to fly. I'm always excited when I'm going to the airport, ready to get on an airplane and fly somewhere. Another way of determining your passion is by figuring out what irks and annoys you.

Why's that important?

Because God puts you and I here to solve a problem. We are God's solution to a present problem in the Earth, and we are designed to demonstrate who He is in the capacity that we have been created for. Consequently, whenever we encounter the problem we were created to solve, we are either annoyed by it, irked by it, angered by it, or it would prompt us to take action. And by taking action, we're playing an active role as a result of a will that is on the inside.

God made the first move. But by aligning with what God wants for us, we are now developing that will to live. So, the will to live isn't just fulfilling something that you wanted to do in terms of, I've always wanted to be this when I grew up, or an active passion or desire. It could be the will or the desire to fix a problem that has been bothering you, causing you sleepless nights, or annoying you to no end.

And, yes, this is the big difference between the constant complainers and the people who take action. The ones who take action are the ones who are living. The one who complains chooses not to live. They're on the sidelines and not taking any active role in seeing life unfold for them. They prefer to be entertained by what's happening around them, but that's not what God wants for you.

God wants you to be in the game. He wants you to take an active role in starting to live by doing something to solve a problem.

Understanding the Value of the Gift of Life

One of the things we would pray for as kids growing up in church is to thank God for the breath of life. Why? Because breathing in and breathing out, even though it seems automatic to us, can easily be taken for granted. But really, we need to remember that the source of our breathing is from God. Now, I wanted to highlight the breath because one of the meanings of the word breath is the word spirit (in the previous chapter). In the Gospel of John, it says that *my words are spirit and they are life.* Now, I want to be very careful that I'm not just taking scriptures all over the place and compacting them together to create some massive theology that may not necessarily be what God is saying.

The time we have on Earth is a gift, but not many people consider it to be so. And as a result, many people do not see life as valuable as it really is.

I've had to deal with a really painful loss of people who passed away in the two weeks preceding the time of this writing.

I first received the news of a lady who was very dear to me. She simply slept and never woke up. Before her demise, she attended the ministry I previously served as associate pastor, and she had been really helpful to my family. When I moved into my new home, this lady poured herself into helping me settle in. She brought delicious food to the housewarming party to ease things for me. She was the epitome of the true definition of love, and her demise really struck my family badly.

About a week after this lady's death, we received the news of the death of a fellow Black pilot. There are only about 100 of us Black pilots in the airline I work with (out of over 5,000 pilots). So, the news of his death sent a major shockwave our way. The sad thing is that he died snorkeling while on a work trip, leaving his companion and two beautiful children behind.

Hearing of these deaths – and still trying to process the whole thing – gives me more reasons to appreciate this life that I have. I am in no way better than that beloved lady who's passed on. Neither am I more privileged than that pilot. I take it that it is only by God's mercy that I have not been consumed.

So, I do not overstate when I say that time is truly a gift and one that we must all learn to appreciate. It's a gift because to get to where you need to be, you need time. You need time to be able to live and soar. And God, in His kindness, allocates the time to us all. God does so to let you know that He knows you're going to make it to the end. God gives time (and life) to us because He wants us to fulfill that purpose for which He created us and also lets us know He's always on our side.

However, merely acknowledging that life is a gift may not be enough to show that we appreciate that gift. We respond to it, and our response will be to live that life to its fullest.

I think it's the right moment to say that the essence of this book is to help you show God how grateful you really are for the life you have received. Now, that's because when you live to soar, you are showing God how much you appreciate the life you have. When you make the decision to live up to the fullness of the gift of God's breath and word over you, you tell Him that you do not take His precious gift to you for granted.

One question for you. How grateful have you been for the gift of life you have? And how exactly have you been expressing that gratitude to God?

Well, you can start by revisiting the part just before this one and then make the choice to live.

SECTION 2

Soar

CHAPTER 4
HAVE A GOAL, THEN A PLAN

Start with The Goal

What's 'living to soar' going to mean to you?

Or what exactly is that thing that, when you achieve it, will show that you are successful and living according to God's purpose for you?

Can you say it in three sentences? How about one sentence? How about in three words? Do you even have it written somewhere?

Now, do you have a picture of what your life would look like when you eventually get to that point in your life?

In his book, *The Seven Habits of Highly Effective People,* Steve Covey explains that if you want to be effective in life, the number one habit you need to have is to always start a process with the end in mind.

So, I wanted to be a pilot. But I did not merely find myself flying airplanes after a few years of wishing to be a pilot. What happened was that I had always had a picture of me flying airplanes. Each time I walked through the streets of my imagination, I'd always see myself flying jets and welcoming my passengers on board. It did take a while, though, but that end I always had in mind is what I'm doing now.

So, why do you even need a goal?

Picture this. It's a crispy, clear Sunday afternoon. You just returned from church and had lunch. You go to your closet, pick out a nice outfit, fix your hair and face, and slide your feet into a pair of comfy shoes. You pick up your car keys and set off to the front door (or garage, if you have one). Then, your spouse asks you where you're going.

And you're like, "I don't know, I'll just drive out and see."

Well, a number of things are likely going to happen to you. You'll either drive down to the nearest store or entertainment center and spend a few (unplanned) hours there. Or you could keep driving in circles around your block. Or worse still, you could set off driving hours and hours away from home, with no plan to keep your engine running when you're out of gas and realize that you're really heading NOWHERE. And if your friend finds you on the way and asks for a ride to the town square, you are more likely to oblige because you're not really going anywhere.

Sadly, this is just how it is when we say we want to soar with no definite goal in mind. You may put in all the effort you can and eventually become very busy. But if there is no goal (or an end in mind), then you aren't really going to get anywhere.

And, of course, having a goal in mind will keep you moving when things become uncomfortable. I've had times during my training when I was almost overwhelmed with all that was required of me to achieve my dream. However, the goal of becoming an airline pilot kept me in the process. Whenever I picture myself in control of an airplane, I get reminded and motivated to want to continue in the process.

Look at Jesus, our perfect example, in Hebrews 12:2

Looking unto Jesus the author and finisher of our faith; who for the joy that was set before him endured the cross, despising the shame, and is set down at the right hand of the throne of God.

The shame and pain of the cross was not something Jesus enjoyed. And in

Jesus's day, being hung on a cross was considered the most shameful and demeaning way to die. Families even went as far as renouncing any member who was to be punished by hanging on a cross in order to preserve their name. But despite how shameful it was, Jesus endured it all because of the joy that was set before him.

What was the joy?

The church was going to be born. Mankind would be saved. God would redeem mankind. The devil would be defeated. Sin would be conquered. Access to God would be granted. The veil would be torn from top to bottom. Jesus did not care about all that stuff he had to deal with, the piercing of His side, the nails, and the humiliation. Though He was concerned at one point, do you know what Jesus did? He spent time in prayer because his focus was on the fact that the will of the Lord had to be done. He set the image of the will of God being fulfilled before Him all the time and was able to endure the cross because of that.

If you cannot picture yourself actually doing the thing that you've dreamt about or that thing God has instilled in you, you'll be more likely to quit. It's somewhat inevitable. That's why it makes no sense to start anything that you haven't seen yourself completing. Because when opposition comes, there'll be nothing to keep you from giving in.

How do I know the opposition will come? The truth remains that wherever God's Word has been sent, whenever the Word is released, things will come to test the Word. So, if you received that goal from the Word of God to you, opposition will surely arise against it. But you will overcome when you keep that word (as an end) before you at all times.

Lastly, having a specific goal saves you from wasting your life on distractions.

When Jesus therefore perceived that they would come and take him by force, to make him a king, he departed again into a mountain himself alone.

In John 6:15, the people wanted to make Jesus a king. He was wise, and they supposed He would make a good and fearless leader. And well, being a king wouldn't have been a bad thing for Jesus. He would even be able to reach more people and heal more of them. Towns and villages will no longer dishonor Him and send Him out of their land, and many will want to listen to Him. But that was not the reason He came to the Earth.

If Jesus hadn't put the vision of salvation before His face all the time, He might have given in to the distraction of becoming a man-made king instead of a God-sent messiah.

When you have a goal or vision for your journey, you will not stop at every junction. You will not expend your energy, money, and life on everything that passes by. You will be better able to say no to things that do not count toward your goal. You will be a bit more intentional about bringing that vision to pass by sticking only with the things that help you achieve that goal.

Now, A Plan

As great as having a vision or a goal is, it is not enough. How are you going to get there? How are you going to move from where you are to where the goal or vision says you should be?

When you receive a vision from God about the kind of life He wants you to live, you obviously need to create a plan for executing that vision.

But shouldn't God also figure out how to bring His Word to pass?

Well, yes. It is God's responsibility to breathe His Word into us and also empower that Word to manifest. But we also have a responsibility to respond and plan towards the fulfillment of that goal because God will not impose Himself on us, our schedule, the things we choose to do or not do, and the places we go. Therefore, in making a plan for your goal, it means that you are going to schedule time for working on that vision, do the necessary things to realize that vision, gather the knowledge needed for that vision, and become the person that can really live in that vision.

Otherwise, a goal without a plan for its execution will only remain wishful thinking. If I hadn't come to the point where I decided to attend aviation school to gain the knowledge I needed to fly an airplane, the vision to become a pilot would have only remained in my head.

WHAT DOES A PLAN DO FOR YOU?
A plan gives you clarity about your goal.

Because we are mortal beings and are bound by time, the visions we receive are usually in parts – one message at a time. But as we move toward the vision we receive from God, we get a clearer picture of the tiny details of that goal.

Having a plan shows you what you need for your process compared to what you already have. From this, you can discern the different components of your vision that need to be put in place for its fulfillment.

It shows you the reality of where you currently are.

Having an actionable plan for your goals is a very elaborate way to really see the reality of your current situation. If your goal is to become a kind, generous, and loving spouse, your plans to get there will help you understand how much kindness, generosity, and love you already have. You'll become more conscious of your show of these virtues so that you can make the necessary effort to fill in any existing gap.

It measures your progress towards your goal.

Without a plan, you may never know how close or far you are from the end you have in mind.

God had an end in mind when He sent His only Son to die for the sins of the world. But that was not all; He had a plan, too. Every detail of this plan is strewn in nearly every book of the Old Testament as prophecies. Jesus knew God's plan, too – as written in the scriptures. So, at different times, when the mob would have killed Jesus, they couldn't because, according to God's plan, it wasn't time yet.

Then they sought to take him, but no man laid hands on him because his hour had not yet come.
John 7:30 KJV

But when the time eventually came for God's vision to come to pass, even Jesus knew and was prepared for it.

Then cometh he to his disciples, and saith unto them, Sleep on now, and take your rest: behold, the hour is at hand, and the Son of man is betrayed into the hands of sinners.
Matthew 26:45 KJV

Can you imagine what would have happened if God did not have a plan for how Jesus was to save the world? What would our fate be today if Jesus did not know that God's plan was that He would die the shameful death of the cross? Without that knowledge, Jesus would probably have let Himself get thrown off a cliff by an angry mob, and all of God's intention to save us would have gone down the drain.

The good thing is that drafting out a plan for executing your goals is not a challenge at all. And if you are as passionate – as I was as a little child – about your goals, then creating a plan for execution should thrill you.

Finally, remember we noted in the early chapters that God's breath is what gives us life, and to live to soar means to live life to the fullest and according to God's will. So, it will not be out of place to do the planning with God. If He'll be the one to judge the outcome of the life you eventually decide to live, it would be a great idea to get the plan from Him as well.

CHAPTER 5

THE PRISON OF NOSTALGIA AND THE FEAR OF THE UNKNOWN.

There are two things that can distract you or put you in neutral as they relate to your will or desire to live. One is the prison of nostalgia, which deals with your past. The second is the fear of the unknown, which deals with your future.

In Numbers 13, the children of Israel get on God's nerves. But Chapter 12 is where Moses sends the 12 spies into the promised land to go spy out the land. He selects 12 leaders, one from each tribe. They go into the promised land to discover how fruitful the land is. They discovered how big the grapes were, so much that a cluster was so big and heavy that they had to tie it to a pole, and two men had to carry it back into the camp in the wilderness. When they finally arrived at the camp to give the report, 10 of the spies gave a negative report. They go along the lines of, "Yes, the land is good, but there are giants in the land, and we saw the descendants of Anak, and we are like grasshoppers in their sight."

Now, whenever you use the conjunction but, you're basically negating anything that was said prior to it. On the other hand, two of the spies, Joshua and Caleb, were announcing, "Let's go conquer this at once. If God says it's ours, we can take it. We got this, right?" But the others kept saying, "No, we can't because we will be destroyed."

Now, here is my emphasis on the prison of nostalgia. Most of the children of Israel wept and lifted up their voices to ask Moses why he brought them out there. They also lamented that God brought them out to kill them. Their concern wasn't for themselves alone. They were also afraid that their children would not have a future anymore. Now, that's the fear of the unknown.

Let's talk about nostalgia. Because of the fear of the unknown, the children of Israel started saying, let's make ourselves a new leader who will take us back to Egypt – an experience they've had before, whose outcome seemed better than what lay ahead, which they did not know.

Here's the problem with nostalgia. The anatomy of the human heart is very unique. Its electrical impulses are hundreds and thousands of times stronger than those of the brain. This is why you can find yourself thinking one thing, but because the heart feels what it wants to feel, it can override your brain and logical thinking. And then you find yourself doing something that your mind has been telling you all along not to do. And then, when you're asked why, your response would be, "I don't know. I kept telling myself that I shouldn't do this, or I shouldn't go in this direction, or I shouldn't say this, but then it just happened. It just came out."

The strength of the heart's impulses is the same reason the Bible says we need to guard our heart because out of it flows the issues of life. When you speak, act, behave, or function out of the genuineness of your heart, you give out of your strength at those points. It's not fake anymore. Your brain can think things, but your heart might feel a different way. But if you're disciplined enough to override your heart, you should be able to be cordial in your actions when your heart wants to do otherwise, especially during times of intense emotional distress.

However, in many ways, the brain can temper with the genuineness of who you are. But when you are a person who does things from the sincerity of your heart, there's no holding back, no denying, and no hiding of who you are. So, guarding your heart is, in essence, twofold. One, you watch what goes into your heart (what you expose yourself to) because the heart does not think for itself; you have to train it. However, once you've trained your heart to feel, act, or respond in a certain way, it goes on autopilot, and it becomes very hard to override it.

We all know how God delivered the children of Israel from Egypt. But because of what they were hearing and the fear of the unknown, they resorted to the prison of nostalgia. They started to think back on how things used to be in the past. They began to see good in their past in Egypt. Of course, they were not thinking about slavery. They were not thinking about being in bondage and under wicked taskmasters. All they thought about were leeks and onions, the things that now appeared good about their past, and they thought their lives were better in slavery. All because of the unknown.

Think about it. How many times have you found yourself thinking about an unpleasant situation or relationship you just came out of, and you start to remember and wish for all the good moments? You forget the toxicity, the bad things that happened, and all the times you felt abused, disrespected, or used. You only selectively remember the few good moments you had in that situation, and you want to go back to it. That's the prison of nostalgia; it's selective memory and is misleading.

Do you know why?

Selectively remembering the good times over the overwhelming bad makes your heart gravitate toward the situation, circumstance, or person involved. You want to experience those good moments again, forgetting that with that person or situation comes the unpleasantness that made you leave in the first place.

From another perspective, the prison of nostalgia may not have to do with a bad situation. It may simply have to do with God asking you to leave something that feels good at the moment with the promise of something better. In this case, the prison of nostalgia happens when you really cannot let go of what feels good now to trust God for what lies ahead. The saying that you cannot drive to your destination constantly looking at your rear-view mirror is so valid when you're dealing with the prison of nostalgia. You can't go forward constantly looking back. You cannot live to soar when you're always focused on the things in your past. You will either hit something, hurt yourself, or lose your sense of direction.

Apostle Paul is a perfect example of someone who did not let himself stay bound by the prison of nostalgia.

Circumcised the eighth day, of the stock of Israel, of the tribe of Benjamin, an

Hebrew of the Hebrews; as touching the law, a Pharisee; concerning zeal, persecuting the church; touching the righteousness which is in the law, blameless. But what things were gain to me, those I counted loss for Christ. Yea doubtless, and I count all things but loss for the excellency of the knowledge of Christ Jesus my Lord: for whom I have suffered the loss of all things, and do count them but dung, that I may win Christ.
Philippians 3:5-8 KJV

In Philippians 3, Apostle Paul makes it clear that he indeed had a 'good life' before he received Christ. He was born a Jew. He was a Pharisee who knew all 613 laws of Moses and was taught by Gamaliel, the best instructor in his field of expertise at the time. But Paul would rather take his boast in Christ, leaving behind the seemingly good achievements he had made in life so he could gain Christ. He chose not to be trapped and limited by the good in his past.

For me, I've served in ministry as a pastor and Minister of Music. I've been part of album creations and choir competitions. In addition to that, I've worked for several airlines, and I am currently a captain of the airline I work with. I make a decent salary, and I own a decent house, all of which are great. But I am willing to lay all of that down so that I might win the prize that God has for me, which is the high calling of God in Christ Jesus.

When it comes to the will to live and living to soar, what is it about your past (or present) that you need to lay down so you can get to where God wants you. Could it be your culture? Your paradigm? A pedestal you found yourself on? A situation you've been in? Ways you've been taught? Or things you may have learned that may have been good for that moment or helpful in bringing you to where you are now?

Whatever the prison of nostalgia may be for you, know that the moment you choose to let go of it is when you truly begin to live, ready to soar.

The Fear of the Unknown

The future can be quite scary. But the most frightening part is that every step you take and everything you experience is part of the process your life needs to truly make sense. Just as you cannot graduate from college without meeting all the requirements of the school, you cannot skip any of life's processes. Irrespective of what your preferences may be, you have to be willing to go through the processes life will demand for you to soar.

But there's good news. You won't be doing any of those processes alone. As a matter of fact, you cannot do them by yourself.

When thou passest through the waters, I will be with thee; and through the rivers, they shall not overflow thee: when thou walkest through the fire, thou shalt not be burned; neither shall the flame kindle upon thee.
Isaiah 43:2 KJV

As a Christian, you will go through the different phases of life with God right by your side, guiding you all the way. He is with you every step of the way – no matter how bleak the future may look. Do you know why? God knows the way you should go and the direction you should take. He knows every obstacle that you'll have to face and what the enemy will try to do to take you out. But He is standing right there to protect, keep, and help you get through those processes because on the other side of the process is that thing, that assignment, that goal, that purpose, that place where you start to soar.

CHAPTER 6
SOARING DOESN'T HAPPEN OVERNIGHT

As an airline pilot, I fly airplanes that can hold up to 200 people, excluding the crew. But that's not all; I also fly long distances. I can go 3,000 miles plus at a time. So, we're talking six, seven, and even up to eight hours of flight on each trip. I can do that now, and I'm grateful for that. I can also visit different destinations around the world and not buy a ticket for any trip – instead, I get paid to go to these places.

However, I did not start flying complex planes and long distances immediately after I got out of aviation school. In fact, my first flight was a Cessna 172, and I was 18 and in college at the time. It was a discovery flight.

I flew the Cessna 172 for about 35 minutes. It was a very short flight, but it was one of the most breathtaking 35 minutes of my life – living in the dream I've had since I was a kid. During the flight, my trainer taught me a lot of practical stuff about airplanes. He started off by showing me how to walk around and inspect the plane before any trip. We inspected the fuel tanks, checked for any sign of damage on the aircraft, and made sure it was safe for the skies. Then we got to flying. He first showed me how to start the airplane.

As we were taxiing, he demonstrated different things to me and then allowed me to do some of them. When it was time to take off, he also allowed me to do that. Then, I practiced doing some turns while we were in the air. We climbed up to about 3,000 feet, and I was in control most of the time. Then, when it was time to land, he showed me how, and I landed the plane safely.

Was I nervous throughout that flight?

Yes.

I had never flown an airplane before, even though being an airline pilot was the peak of my definition of soaring at the time. I had to have a first experience that would eventually usher me into other experiences within the process.

Fast forward to today, and now I've made flights to London, Paris, and Amsterdam on an airplane that's far more complex than the Cessna172. It's no longer me and an instructor anymore. Now, I am the captain of the flight, and I am responsible for an entire airplane with between 100 to 200 passengers and 6 or 7 other crew members. So, I'm the one in charge. Moreover, the planes I fly now are worth about three thousand times the cost of the plane I flew the very first time!

Getting to where I currently am wasn't easy. It was a journey. And more importantly, it required a process.

I had to start with the desire to become a pilot and a passion for flying airplanes. I had to nurture my passion to travel to different destinations and get paid to do it. I had to go to an aviation school to learn all the technicalities involved in flying an airplane. I also had to go through practical training to be able to use everything I've learned.

Now, I took the time to explain (maybe not in great detail) the process I had to undergo to become the Captain I am today so that I can drive home my point. Soaring does not happen overnight – it requires a process. Sometimes, that process can take as long as a few months to a few years or a few decades (like mine), depending on how and where it's happening.

But no matter how long it takes for you to get to the point of soaring, there's one thing you should never lack on your journey to soaring. That one thing is faith.

Wherefore seeing we also are compassed about with so great a cloud of witnesses, let us lay aside every weight, and the sin which doth so easily beset us, and let us run with patience the race that is set before us,
Hebrews 12:1 KJV

Have you ever wondered what this sin that easily besets us and why we ought to lay it down so that we can succeed in the race that is set before us?

Could it be lying? Laziness? Gossiping? Or maybe a lack of a consistent prayer life?

Before we can figure that out, look at the first word in this first verse – wherefore. Whenever you see that word at the beginning of any sentence in the Bible, it means that whatever precedes it is relevant to understanding the sentences that follow. So, to understand what sin is, we must consider what the previous chapter (Hebrews 11) talks about. It talks about faith and characters who underwent their journeys with great faith.

Also, if you look, from the beginning (Genesis 3), at the sin that first slowed man down, you'll find that this sin is unbelief. We should never get to a point on our journey where we begin to doubt God or our ability to soar. We must embark on our journeys with faith in our hearts.

Why You Need Faith for Your Journey

The first reason you need faith to soar is so that you will be able to receive the Word of God concerning that future you're aspiring to have. This is because that which comes out of God's mouth concerning you is what He knows and believes about you. If you are going to lead a group of people in ministry, God already thought that about you, and so He spoke that over your life before you even got here. You need to believe what God believes about you.

Before I formed thee in the belly I knew thee, and before thou camest forth out of the womb, I sanctified thee, and I ordained thee a prophet unto the nations.
Jeremiah 1:5 KJV

The fact that you were already in God's mind means that it wasn't just your physical or biological existence God had in mind before you materialized on Earth. He also had the impact you will make on the Earth in mind. He already knew the course you would take in life and what soaring would mean to you.

All that God says (and has determined) over your life is what He believes about you. But what guarantees that God's plan and word for your life come to pass and you eventually live to soar is what you believe about what God has said concerning you. If you do not believe the Word of God that breathes life into your future, soaring is going to be nearly impossible for you to attain.

Clearly, the desire I've nurtured towards flying (since I was a kid) did not just come from a random source. It came from God, and every step of the way, I've had to believe in His perfect plans for me. I've had to trust that He has my best interest at heart and that His Word will not fail.

Secondly, it does not matter how old or young you are. You can only go as high as your level of faith. If your faith gets to a particular level and you don't have the faith to believe beyond that, that's how high you're going to get. And that's because your faith level determines how much of what you have on your inside you can unlock for the assignment God has committed to you.

When you get to a point where you're struggling with your faith, this is the borderline where you start to become afraid of the unknown. It is the point where things start to concern you, and you'll begin to doubt if you can really trust God to go as far as He has said.

The third reason you need faith for your journey is that you will encounter obstacles on your way. Well, sometimes, when we meet obstacles on our journey, it's a bit easy to get carried away by them, and we start to think, *maybe God is against this. Maybe I'm not going to succeed in this. This may be the end of the road.*

But when we have built our faith in God for our process, we will be able to hold on to His promises. Faith in God will help us not to resent Him when those obstacles start to show up. We'll remember His Word and promises and know that He will always help us. Just as in Isaiah 43:2:

When thou passest through the waters, I will be with thee; and through the rivers, they shall not overflow thee: when thou walkest through the fire, thou shalt not be burned; neither shall the flame kindle upon thee.

God did not say our process would be smooth and easy, like a walk in the park. He did not say we would not encounter obstacles. Instead, God assures us that when we go through the fire, it will not burn us, and the water will not drown us. He's assured us that no matter what comes our way, if He has given us His Word to soar, then we should trust the process because He will surely bring it to pass.

Training an Eaglet to Soar

When we talk about the word 'soaring,' there's just one animal that comes to mind, the eagle. Coincidentally, how an eagle learns to soar is a good analogy to buttress the fact that soaring (in life) is definitely something that requires a process.

So, let me share how an eagle teaches its babies to fly – and eventually soar.

As soon as a mother eagle notices that it is time for her chicks to hit the skies, she takes them, one at a time, and flies up to a high altitude. Then, she shifts herself away from the eaglet and allows it to drop. The baby, in a bid to survive, would then instinctively let out and put their wings to use. But if the eaglet is still unable to fly, the other parent picks it up and returns it to the nest to try again at a later time.

Well, sometimes God sends some people into your life to help you learn to soar with the resources He has deposited in you. In the beginning, these people may not look like they have your best interest at heart – just as I'm sure an eaglet would think its parent wants to kill it by dropping it off a great height. But when you eventually start to soar because of the influence of these people, you will realize how impactful they are to your process, the same way the eaglet realizes its parents' true intentions when it finds itself gliding in the sky.

However, if after several tries, the baby still hasn't learned to use its wings, the mother resorts to the next line of training – removing the nest. She starts to gradually take off parts of the nest until the eaglet no longer has anything to hold on to. This spurs the smaller bird to fly for survival.

Think about it. The comfort zone is usually an enemy to soaring. When you have everything all nice and cozy, there's usually no push to go beyond the box. But hey, we all know how tough things can get the moment those things that bring comfort are taken away. But sometimes, taking away those things that keep you from seeing the vastness of the sky serves as a good way to begin the process of soaring.

The Place of Teachers and Mentors

Soaring takes time, and there are no shortcuts. Hence, it is important to follow through with all the steps you'll need to soar. Trying to skip or bypass any process will only lead you to sell yourself short. Now, I know you're wondering how you get to navigate the mistakes and portholes in each process successfully if you're not allowed to miss a step.

This is where teachers and mentors come in. You get to learn and glean from their experiences so that you don't necessarily have to go through the tough roads as they did. You get to stand on the shoulders of what they have learned so that you can make progress toward your destination.

Utilizing the Thermals

While you can leverage the experiences of your teachers and mentors, there's also a place for leveraging other things around you for a smooth soar. Remember the eaglet? Even when it does start flying, it may begin by flapping its wings with all its might. With time, it will surely get exhausted and can no longer stay in the air. But that's not the case with its parents. The parents are experienced in soaring, and they know how to utilize the features of the air to their advantage so that they spend minimal energy in the air. *It's called utilizing the wind and thermals (hot air rising to higher altitudes).* All the eagle has to do is spread its wings and allow the thermals to keep it afloat in the air.

This same principle applies to gliders – airplanes with no engines. They get towed into the air and released at a certain altitude. Once released, the plane starts to soar by constantly catching these thermals so it can stay in the air.

So, like the eagle and the glider, what are some things (or people) you can leverage around you to help you soar in life – so you do not end up using up your entire being while doing so?

Pick the lessons

Setbacks are bad, especially while they're happening. They are never pleasant experiences. But if you can get out of a setback or see its end, then it means there is hope and lessons to learn from the experience.

So, whenever you go through a setback, resist the urge to want to dwell on its cause or the way it made you feel. What you should do is to critically look at the setback and see where you can do better next time. Repentance – if the setback resulted from disobedience or unbelief – is a good way to pick lessons from a setback.

So, maybe you had that setback because you did not trust God enough and made hasty decisions on your own. Or you could have set off on the wrong foot after you received word from God about your life or something you should be doing. Or you probably trusted someone with your heart without getting God's approval about them. Learn the lessons and move on.

Try again – and harder

Soaring does not happen overnight. In fact, it can be a life-long process. If so, we definitely cannot let setbacks deter us from truly living to soar.

A good example would be my assignment as a pastor and minister in the church. This isn't something I plan to do for a few years or maybe for twenty years, and then I'd stop working in the Lord's house. No, the goal is to keep serving until God calls me home. So, if I happen to face something that impacts my pastoral assignment – like I did in chapter one, I won't stop ministry because of that. Instead, I would repent, make the changes required of me, and move on. That's what God wants you to do, too.

You Do Not Have to Solve Every Problem

Apart from setbacks, something else that can hold you back from getting to that point where you start to soar is distractions. I know when we talk about distractions, we quickly think about Instagram, Facebook, and all those social media platforms. Yes, those are major distractions – especially for this generation.

I'd love to buttress this point with the development of a baby. After babies are born, they do not immediately start to see and understand the things around them. It takes them a few days to begin to make sense of the interactions of light around them. With time, they begin to see clearly and even start to stare and be in awe of everything happening around them. And even when they start to see clearly, they cannot make total sense of everything around them, and that is perfectly okay. While a parent can simultaneously make sense of the things happening around the home and on the TV, the baby can only understand its crib, the ceiling, its milk bottle, and mommy and daddy's touch. And the emphasis? Nobody is hurrying the baby to understand anything beyond what they can.

You don't have to solve every problem. If you are going to soar, you should focus on the things or areas that are of immediate concern to you. I promise you, you cannot soar with so much unnecessary baggage. You won't be able to effectively glide your way far enough.

Back to our analogy of the eagle. When the eagle soars, it is only concerned about the wind and the thermals. These two things keep it soaring for long, even when it has to hunt over the sea or a cliff. The eagle does not bother itself with the waves in the water, the ship sailing by, or the height of the cliff over which it flies. Its only concern is the condition of the air.

One way to ensure that you aren't trying to solve everything at once is to set strict priorities for your life. Not everything in your life will matter to the same degree. Some will be critical to your soaring, and others will only constitute a nuisance for you. Pay attention to the essentials only. Other times, trying not to solve everything may actively involve your having to cut your losses.

I am the true vine, and my Father is the husbandman. Every branch in me that beareth not fruit he taketh away: and every branch that beareth fruit, he purgeth it, that it may bring forth more fruit.
John 15:1-2 KJV

The pruning process, according to these words of Jesus, involves cutting away things that are not necessary so that the vine and the branch can produce more fruit. When it comes to soaring or reaching the pinnacle of what you're supposed to be doing in life, you'll experience some successes at different points. And in the midst of your processes, you'll need to cut some things from your life so they do not weigh you down as you soar. These cutouts may be friends, habits, paradigms, expectations, and even ways of living.

And the more mature you get on your journey to soaring, the more you know to focus on the things that are necessary for where you're going. Better still, you'll learn to stay in your lane and avoid unnecessary distractions.

But what if I told you that there are some distractions we can easily tick off as good, but are the major things stopping us from soaring? Yes. When you try to stop to solve EVERY single problem that sweeps past you, that becomes a huge distraction to your soaring.

How do you identify distractions?

Is this an urgent need for the goal I want to achieve in life?

What will go wrong if I do not pause everything to solve this problem right now?

Is this something I can delegate to someone else?

So, do not worry (or take abrupt actions) about every problem you encounter as you soar in life. When you do that, you'll have little resources, energy, and zeal for the things that really matter.

CHAPTER 7
CELEBRATE YOUR MILESTONES

It is critical for you to cultivate the habit of celebrating your milestones. Trading in the foreign exchange markets is one of the most unique experiences I've had to learn in life. Luckily, I had the same good friend of mine who got me into it to provide some good wisdom on how to succeed in it.

If I had a good, successful trading day or month, he'd say to me, "Take a portion out of your profit and go spend it on something. It doesn't mean you have to be frivolous, but take something out of it and treat yourself nicely."

At first, I did not understand what this friend of mine was trying to teach me. But much later in life, I came to understand it – he was teaching me to celebrate the milestones in my life.

So, you graduate from elementary school, celebrate that. You graduate from high school, celebrate that. You graduate from college, celebrate that. You have a birthday, celebrate that. You're getting married, obviously, you celebrate that. It's your anniversary, celebrate that. Whatever the milestone may be along your journey in life, take some time to be grateful for it and celebrate yourself for coming that far. You don't have to go overboard. Just something out-of-the-ordinary enough to mark that phase of your life.

In addition to using it as a means to maintain your joy, celebrating every milestone you accomplish is an effective way to encourage yourself. There are a million things in life that will come to discourage you on your journey to soaring. The last thing you want is to be intimidated by any of them.

Celebrating your milestones also helps you remember your why. Why did you start this journey to begin with? Why did you put everything else on hold to embark on this journey? There's no better way to constantly remind yourself of where you're headed than to celebrate whenever you cross a bridge.

CHAPTER 8
GO THE EXTRA MILE

There is no traffic in the extra mile. – Steve Harvey.

Obviously, what I mean by going the extra isn't going beyond your goal or destination. It simply means doing all that it takes to get to your goal.

We may not always realize this, but that extra mile is what is necessary for you to succeed. If you think that just doing the bare minimum is enough, then you're just being average. Going the extra mile takes you beyond the average and puts you into the above-average category. That will then help you succeed even better and even faster than the majority.

Going the extra mile also helps you to soar even higher because there are levels to soaring. A lot of other birds fly, but they cannot soar because they do not go the extra altitudes where soaring truly happens. Chickens can only fly a very short distance, never as high as the pigeons fly. And even at that, a pigeon cannot survive the altitude at which the eagles soar because it does not have the capacity to get there.

What does this imply? The higher you soar, the less congested it is. You won't find pigeons and chickens where the eagle soars. Consequently, by doing the extra, it sets you apart from those that are around you.

The truth remains that while you are the answer to a problem, you are not the only answer. Many are called, but few are chosen. The chosen ones are the ones who answer the call and do whatever it takes to answer that call. So, always go the extra mile. If it takes an hour of prayer every day, go an hour and five minutes or an hour and ten. If it requires a level of study, especially in this day and age of AI, go that extra mile. It will set you apart.

CHAPTER 9
PASS ON WHAT YOU'VE LEARNED.

Our time on earth as individuals may not suffice to fully unpack the entire potential God may intend to unleash on the earth when we fulfill our reason for being created. Hence, it is essential to pass on what we've learned so that others can continue from where we stop.

The importance of passing on what you learn is that it ensures that you leave a legacy, a footprint behind. Secondly, by depositing who you are in others, you are leaving part of who you are in them, thereby multiplying yourself and your influence.

Now there cried a certain woman of the wives of the sons of the prophets unto Elisha, saying, Thy servant my husband is dead; and thou knowest that thy servant did fear the LORD: and the creditor is come to take unto him my two sons to be bondmen. And Elisha said unto her, What shall I do for thee? tell me, what hast thou in the house? And she said, Thine handmaid hath not any thing in the house, save a pot of oil. Then he said, Go, borrow thee vessels abroad of all thy neighbours, even empty vessels; borrow not a few. And when thou art come in, thou shalt shut the door upon thee and upon thy sons, and shalt pour out into all those vessels, and thou shalt set aside that which is full. So she went from him, and shut the door upon her and upon her sons, who brought the vessels to her; and she poured

out. And it came to pass, when the vessels were full, that she said unto her son, Bring me yet a vessel. And he said unto her, There is not a vessel more. And the oil stayed.
2 Kings 4:1-6 KJV

For as long as this widow kept pouring into a vessel, the oil kept increasing. In the same way, you will keep increasing in knowledge and expertise when you dedicate time to pass on what you've learned to others. Never think for one second that by teaching others your "trade secrets," you put yourself at a disadvantage. God is big and resourceful enough to keep pouring in you as you pour into others.

However, in passing on what you've learned, be careful about giving your precious things to those who will not appreciate or are not ready to receive them. But never hold back from passing those gems to those who will receive and value them.

CONCLUSION

I'd like to close out by reminding you that you are graced for this. You have the enablement, the help, and the empowerment to succeed in this life you've been given. In whatever area of your life you see the need to stop to simply survive and really start to live, you have more than enough grace to do that.

All you need to do is submit to your process, put in the necessary effort, and trust the capability of God's presence in you. He has put the pieces back together so you can live. But that's not all. He is also determined to get you to soar. So, go ahead, live to soar!

www.ingramcontent.com/pod-product-compliance
Lightning Source LLC
Chambersburg PA
CBHW060219050426
42446CB00013B/3112